This book belongs to

_____

_____

Welcome to my illustrated world of Steampunk Robots!

Relax and explore a world of whimsical and beautifully detailed pen-and-ink illustrations–all waiting to be brought to life through color.
For artists, mechanics, and robots of all ages.

The artworks in my books are based on illustrations I have drawn over my years as an artist. The designs are filled with imaginative detail whilst remaining fun and accessible to younger colorists.

See more at rjhampson.com

 russelljamesart

Published by Hop Skip Jump
PO Box 1324 Buderim Queensland Australia 4556

First published 2021.
Copyright © 2023 R.J. Hampson.

All Rights Reserved. Without limiting the rights under copyright reserved above, no part of this publication may be reproduced, stored in or introduced into a retrieval system, or transmitted, in any form or by any means (electronic, mechanical, photocopying, recording or otherwise), without the prior written permission of both the copyright owner and the above publisher of this book.
The only exception is by a reviewer who may share short excerpts in a review.

ISBN: 978-1-922472-27-4

Using this book

Find a quiet place away from distractions. Relax and immerse yourself in the process of coloring as you explore the details of each fantastic illustration.

This book is best suited to color pencils or markers. Wet mediums should be used sparingly. Slide a card behind the illustration you are coloring to avoid marker bleed through.

Find fresh coloring pages by signing up to the R.J. Hampson newsletter. Get free downloadable pages and updates on new books at -

rjhampson.com/coloring

ROBOT POLICE DEPARTMENT

MOBILE HOME

CONGESTION

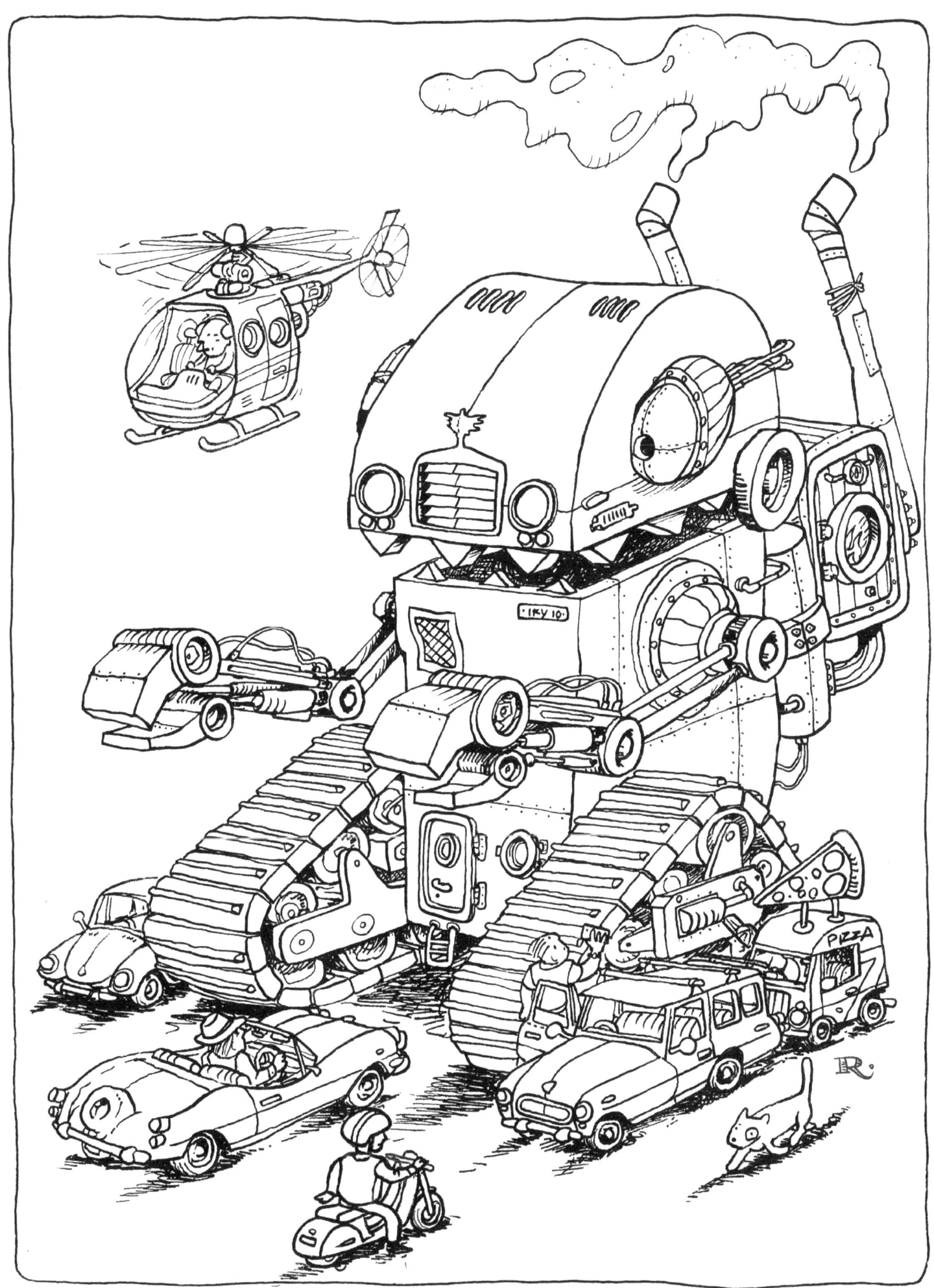

BLIMP-BOT

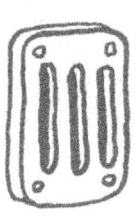

BLIMP-BOT

SENESCENCE

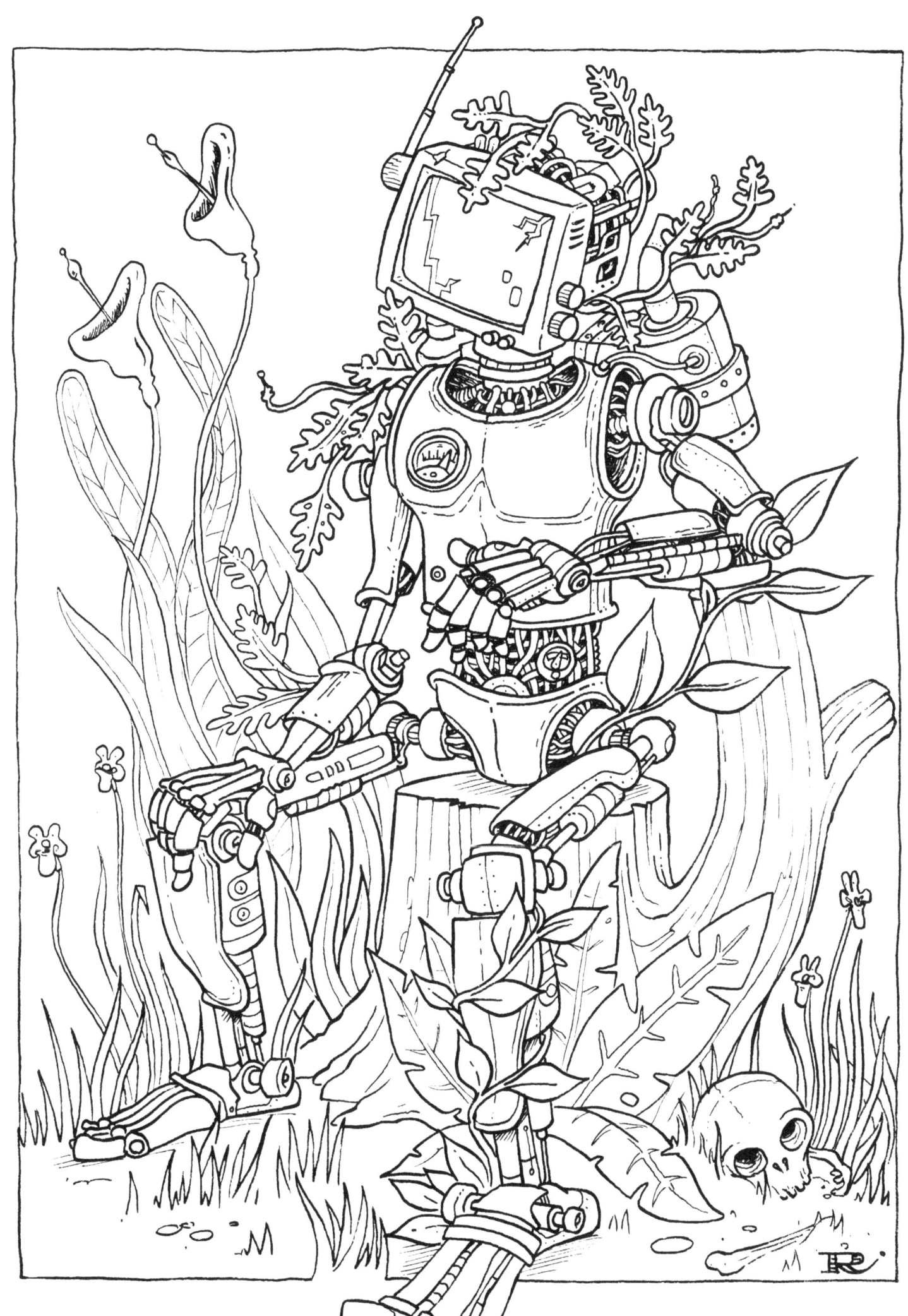

WHEN GOLDFISH RULE THE EARTH

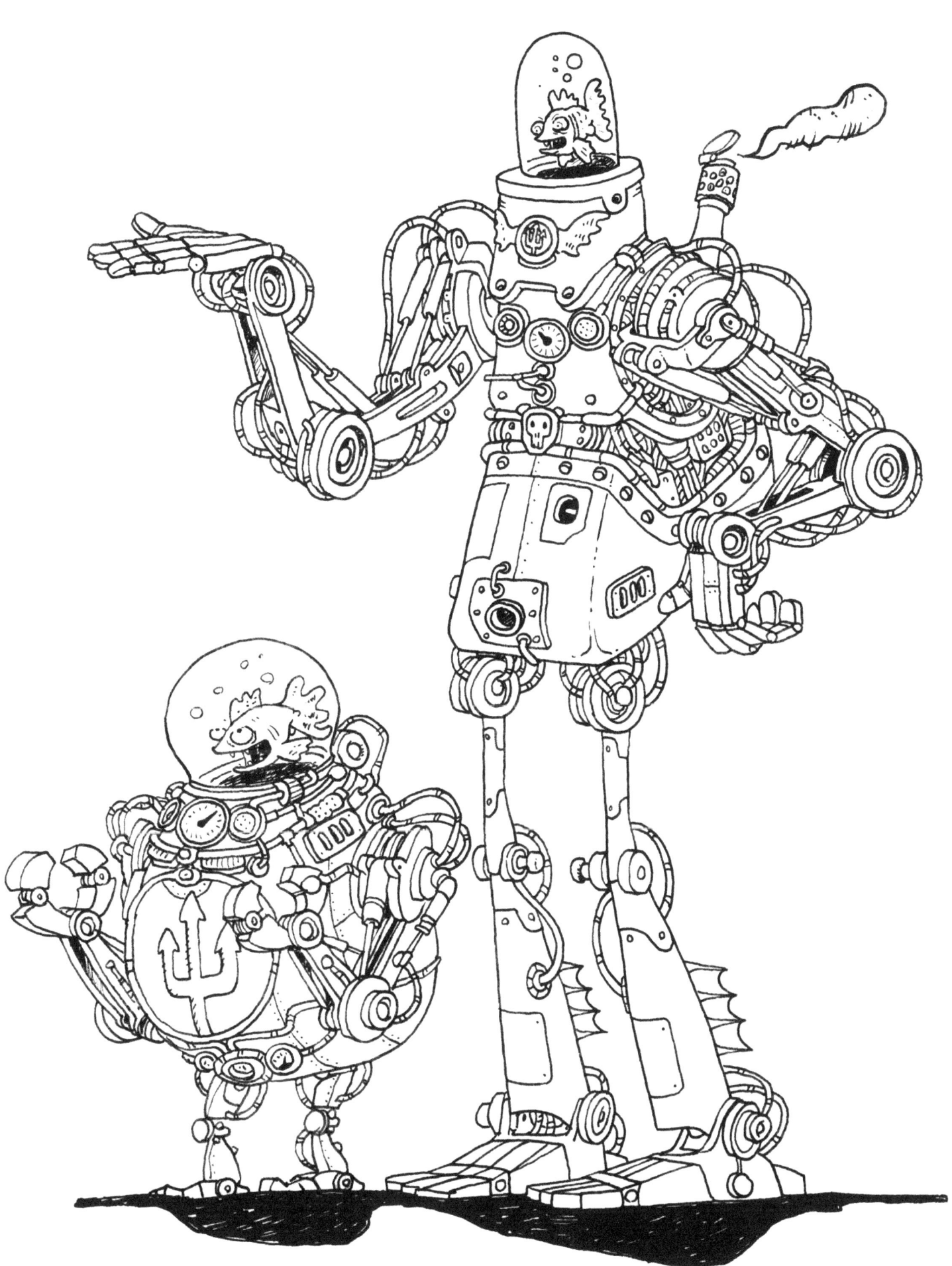

STREETS OF GLORY

STREETS OF GLORY

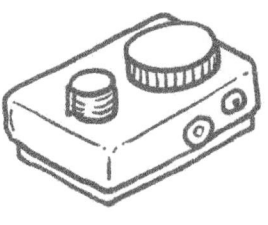

DJ

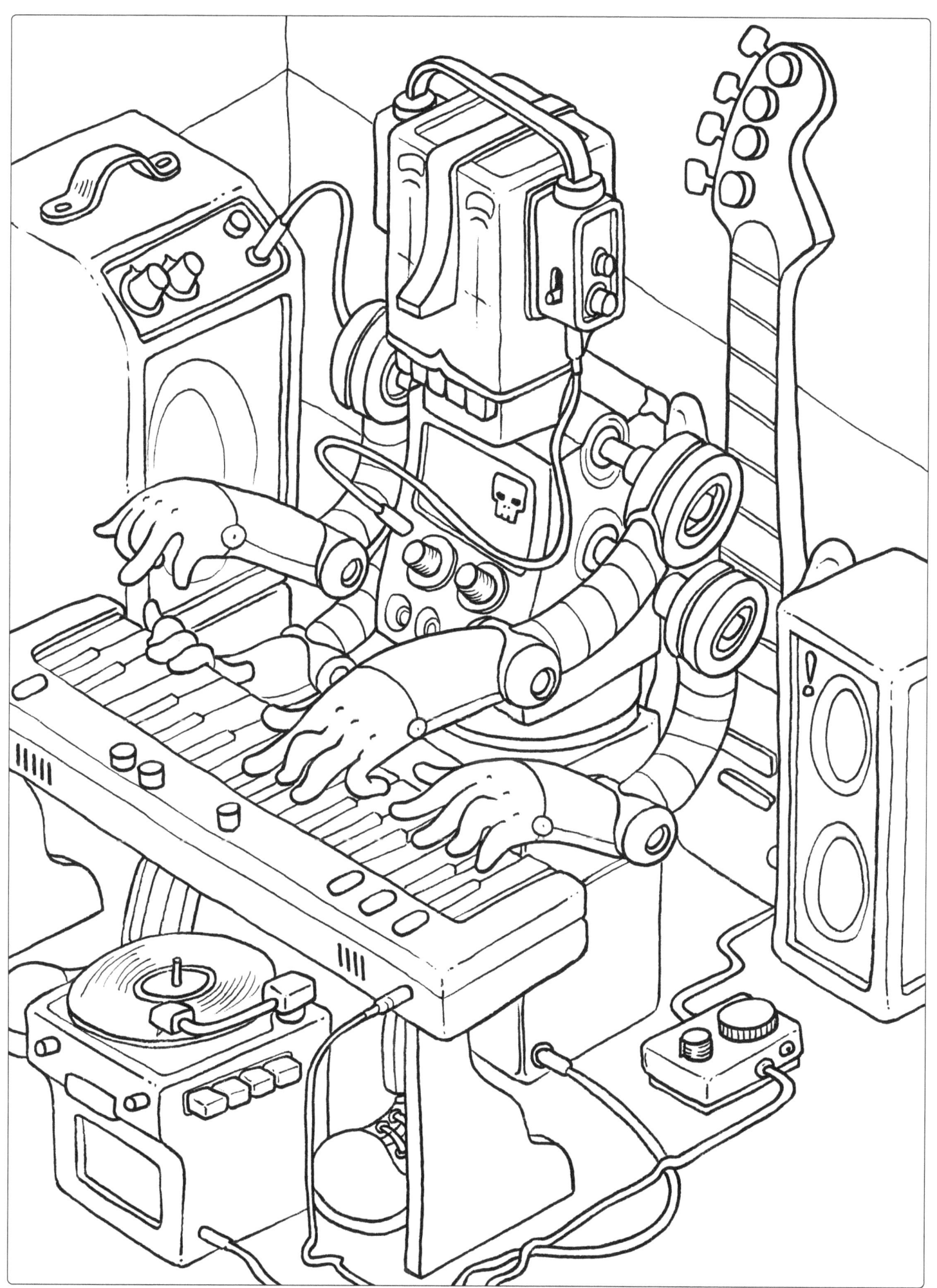

CONSPIRACY

GB-3 GARBAGE DISPOSAL UNIT

GB-3 GARBAGE DISPOSAL UNIT

OFFICE AUTOMATION

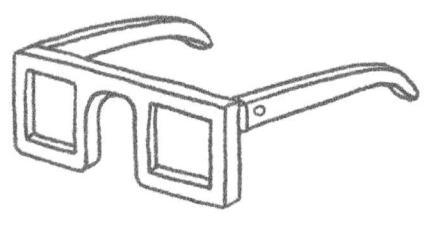

CHEF 2.0

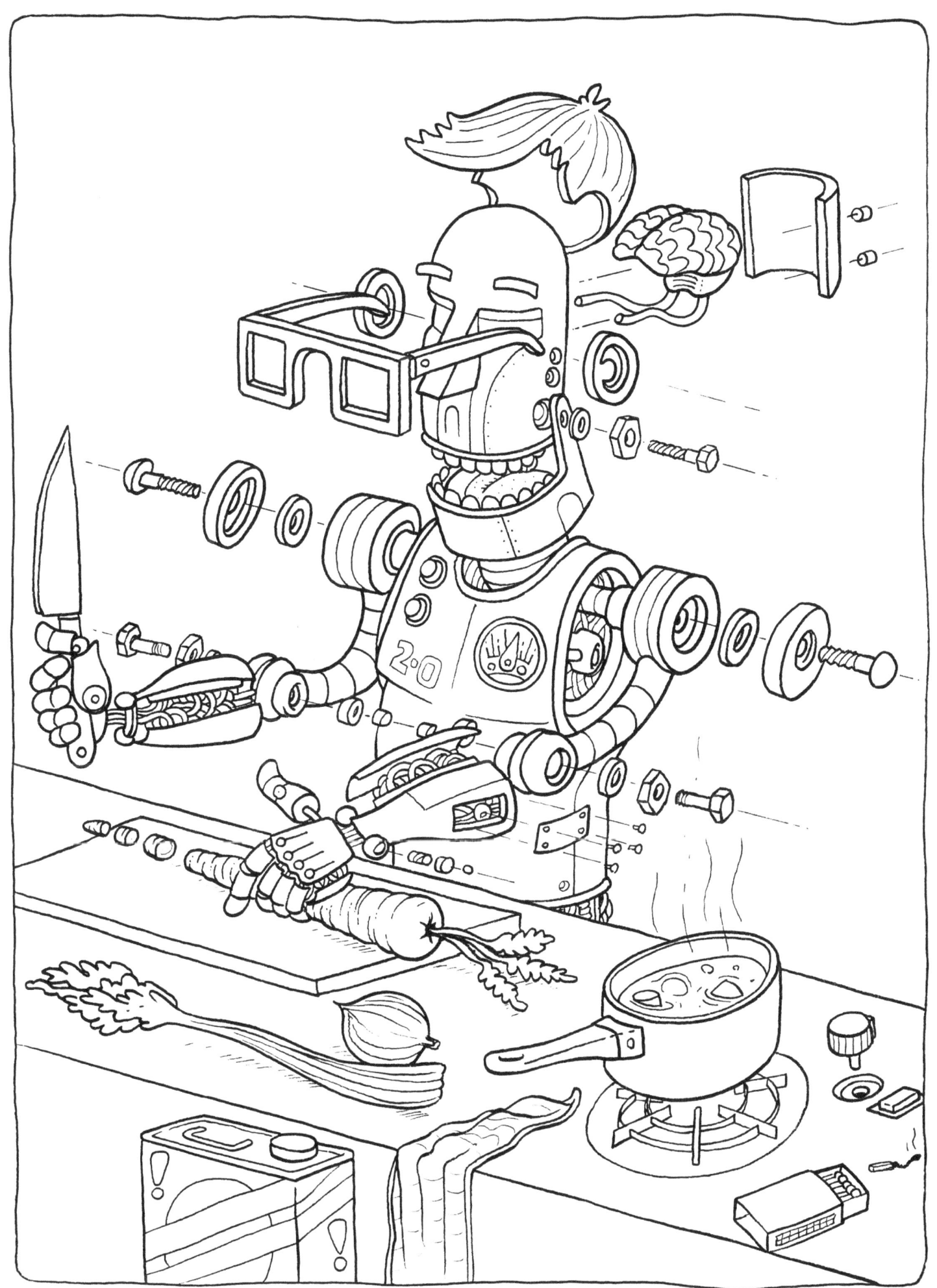

THE JUGGLER

RECHARGE

"WELL, THERE'S YOUR PROBLEM."

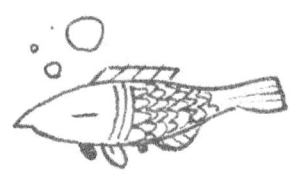

DEEP SEA DIVER

DESERT ROSE

EXPLORATION

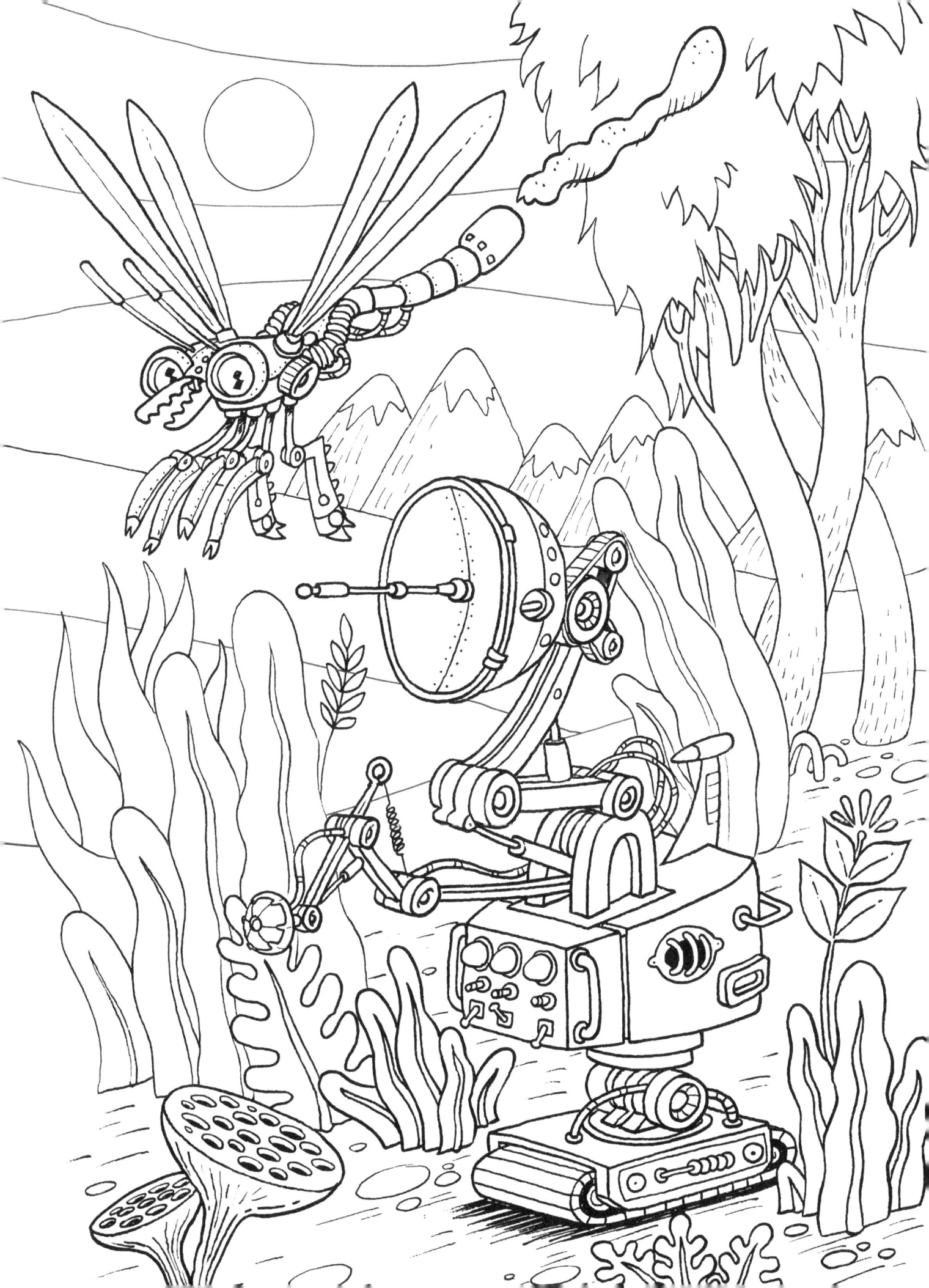

A DAY OUT ON THE TOWN

QU'EST-CE QUE C'EST?

ON THE MOVE

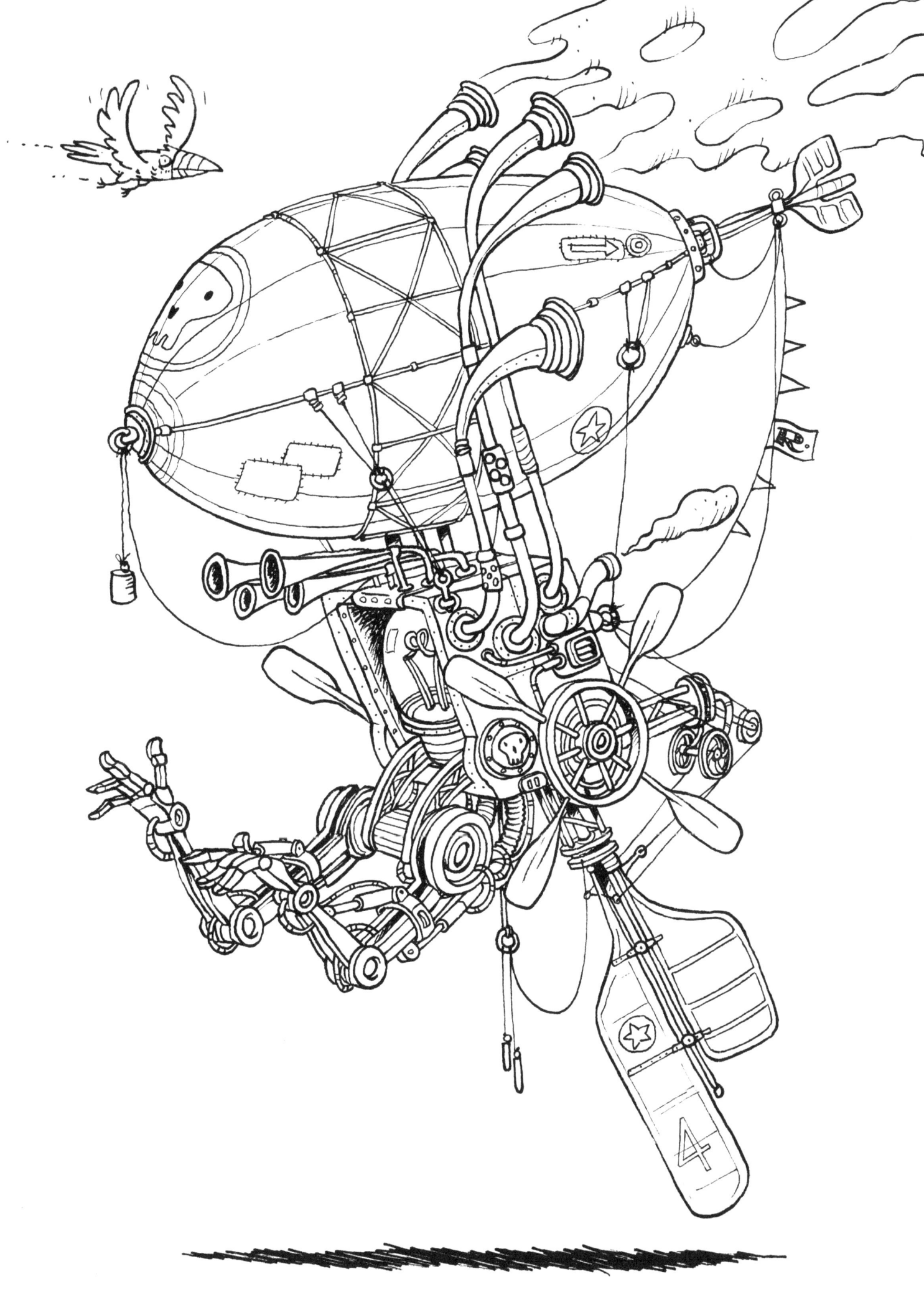

RADIO

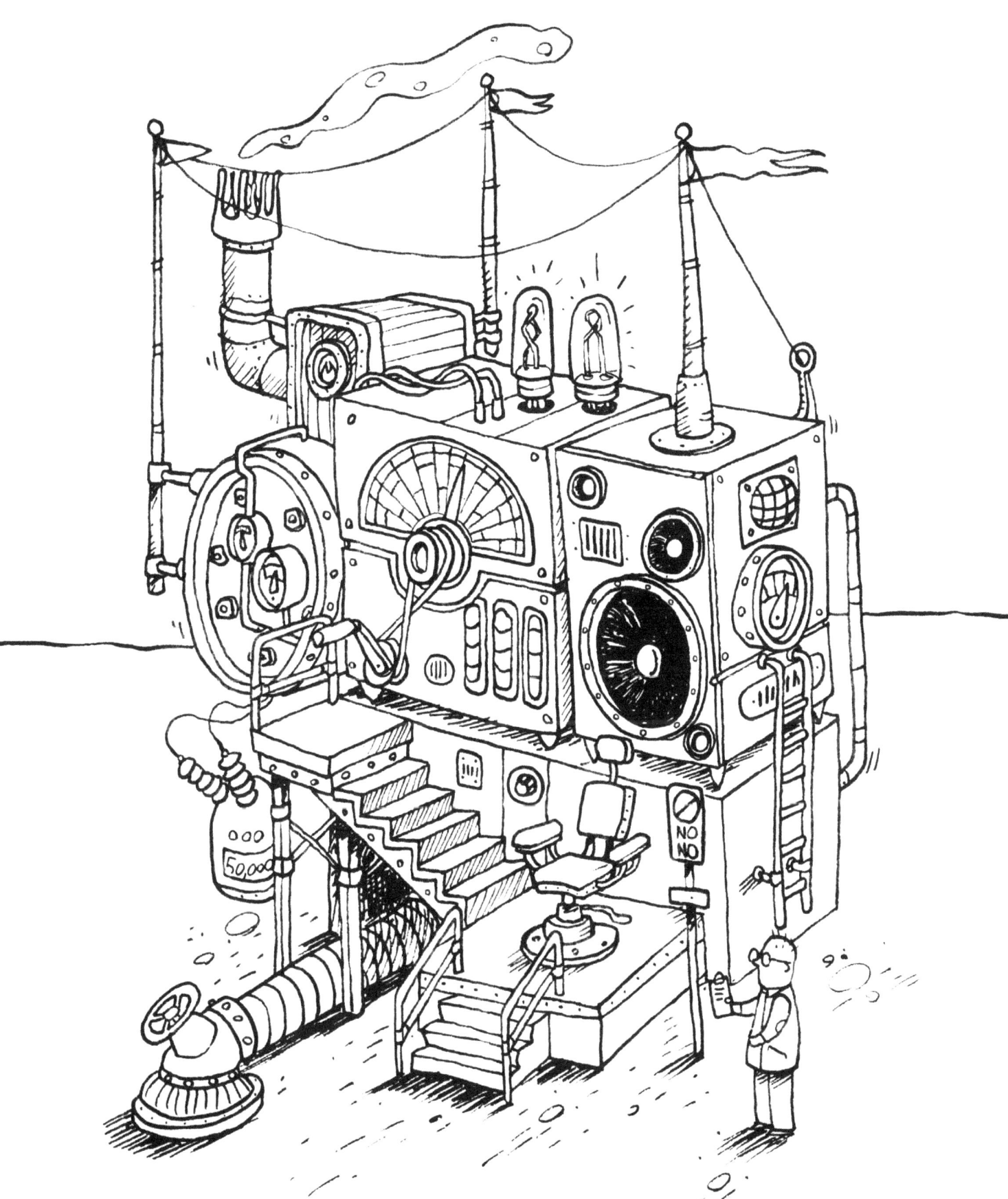

THE P-14

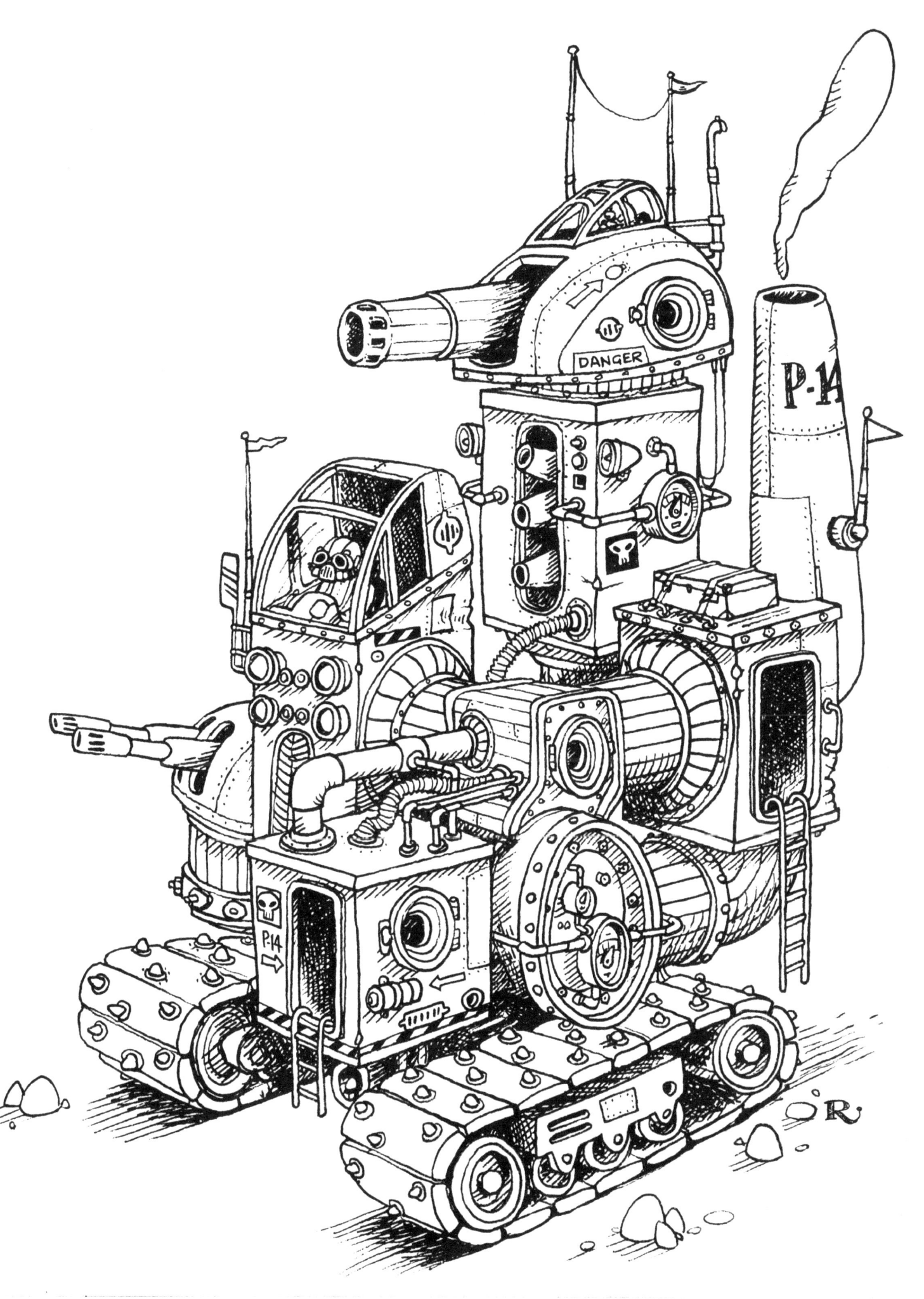

RISE OF THE SNOW GLOBES

ROGUES GALLERY

Discover bonus material!

Find new coloring pages by signing up to Russell's newsletter.
Get free downloadable pages and updates on new books at -
rjhampson.com/coloring

Thanks for choosing this coloring book.
If you enjoyed it, please consider leaving a review.
It will help to let more people in on the experience
plus you'd certainly make this illustrator very happy!

Published books in this series

 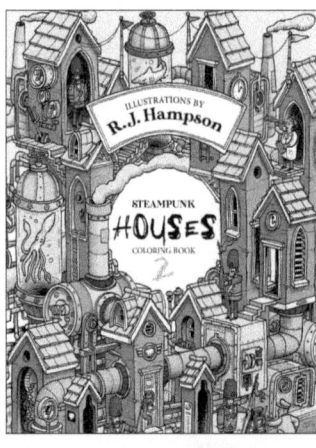  

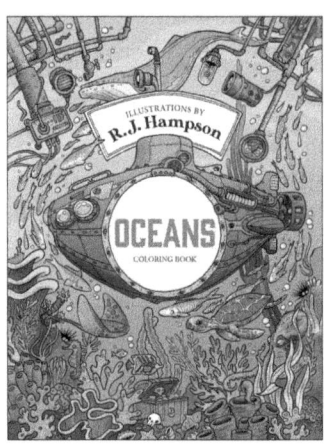   

See flip-throughs and new releases at **rjhampson.com**